OLD MEXICO
An Architectural Pilgrimage

Plate I

STREET SCENE, ZACATECAS

OLD MEXICO
An Architectural Pilgrimage

ALFRED C. BOSSOM

DOVER PUBLICATIONS, INC.
Mineola, New York

Bibliographical Note

This Dover edition, first published in 2004, is an unabridged republication of
the work originally published as *An Architectural Pilgrimage in Old Mexico* by
Charles Scribner's Sons, New York, in 1924.

Library of Congress Cataloging-in-Publication Data

Bossom, Alfred C., 1881–1965.
    [Architectural pilgrimage in old Mexico]
    Old Mexico : an architectural pilgrimage / Alfred C. Bossom.
        p. cm.
    Published in New York in 1924 under title: An architectural pilgrimage in
old Mexico.
    ISBN 0-486-43638-1 (pbk.)
     1. Architecture—Mexico. I. Title.

NA750.B6 2004
720'.972—dc22

                                              2004055141

Manufactured in the United States of America
Dover Publications, Inc., 31 East 2nd Street, Mineola, N.Y. 11501

THIS BOOK IS DEDICATED

TO MY WIFE

WHO ACCOMPANIED ME ON MY TRAVELS

IN MEXICO

AND HELD THE CAMERA IN

MANY INSTANCES

ACKNOWLEDGMENTS

My reason for writing this is the desire to particularly thank Miss Jacqueline Overton for her most painstaking co-operation in the arrangement of the photographs, etc., in this book.

And also, to thank Mr. Harold A. Parker and Mr. H. A. Taylor, and Mr. C. B. Waite of Mexico City, who enabled me to get a number of the photographs.

FOREWORD

ALL that an age signifies is written on the open book of its architecture. The architect is, at best, the conscious recorder of the culture of a race; the thrall of his times. Chief builder he may be, but even though he direct a thousand pairs of skillful hands, he is but the interpreter of the progress and aspirations of his fellowmen. A nation without buildings can leave no vivid transcript of the ideals and temperament of its people.

If one would know the genius of the New World which Columbus gave to Castile and Leon, one must seek those architectural fabrics most typical of the spirit of all the Americas.

Where shall the pilgrim go on such a quest? This is the query which often came to me, a New York Architect of English birth and training, and for years remained unanswered. Surely the soul of America is not truly to be found in its Colonial architecture, which is modified Georgian, in turn founded on Greek and Roman models, through the Italian Renaissance. The search of the United States only called for further study. The aborigines who dwelt within its borders left no architectural remains. They were dwellers in tents of skin, builders of lodges made from poles and boughs. Their materials were temporary, their structural art that of nomads. Even the cliff dwellings of the colorful Southwest are unrelated clusters of dwellings, which owed whatever form they had to conditions which do not carry on. Mounds and tombs and shell heaps abound. Yet what they hold is material only for the archæologist. The architect who would know what America was and is finds in such memorials only ghosts and wraiths. Therefore, the writer, directed by the logic of facts, wandered across the Rio Grande, into that storied land where Montezuma gloried.

Mexico! Not to visit Mexico is not to know the Western Hemisphere. Not to have viewed the monuments of its romantic past is not to sense the inner meaning of American traditions, nor to fully grasp the development of the American people. The traveler who comes to the New World from the mother lands across the seas fails of his mission of understanding if he does not enter this wonder realm where the sun of Hispanic traditions first dawned on the culture horizon of New Spain! To the people of the United States, Mexico is logically a far greater source of influence than has yet been realized or will be until more journeys are made to its ancient fanes. The American architect and the American artist may find much there to kindle their imaginations and inspire their efforts, and the layman also can discover much indeed by making Mexico an inspirational and artistic Mecca.

The art of Aztec and Toltec blended by the free audacious spirit of those old time cultured world wanderers with the ideals of Madrid and Seville, and made sentient by new requirements, still lives in many a stately pile in the republic below the Rio Grande. A reflection of that mighty influence which came with the Spanish conquistadores may be seen, I grant, in the Missions of California and at points in the Southwest, but the true image of the American spirit is revealed best in the country from which Coronado, adventuring, came.

If this account, then, of a pilgrimage to shrines of Mexican architecture shall be the means of inducing others to take up their staffs and go, I shall feel that I have done something, however little, in strengthening the affinities of culture and tradition which unite the Anglo-Saxons and the Latins in a better understanding.

PLATES

PLATES

COURTYARDS

PLATES

PLATES

PORCHES

DOORS

PLATES

PLATES

PLATES

STAIRWAYS

INTERIORS, DETAILS, ETC.

PLATES

OLD MEXICO
An Architectural Pilgrimage

PAINTERS make portraits of individuals, but architects construct the portraits of whole nations. Precedent of course is useful, but not vital, and tradition in the home of the skyscraper is in the making, and in practically all forms of art the American is an eclectic. In this we have very much in common with the Spaniards who originally settled in Mexico.

They were adventurers, crossing the great ocean in little boats, literally taking their lives and fortunes in their hands, willing to brave unknown perils if only they might reach the new country and make for themselves a place therein.

That same spirit is latent in every inhabitant of the United States. The first members of each family to come to America certainly were adventurers, for with the exception of a few personal belongings and their own indomitable spirit, they left everything behind them when they came to this land, with a fixed determination to succeed. Hence life as lived here is subject to more thrills perhaps than anywhere else in the world, but between these thrills come periods of unexciting, strenuous, essential work.

The Spaniards with all their ideas of beauty inherited from tradition-bound Spain found upon their arrival a complete architecture with craftsmanship of a very high standard flourishing in Mexico.

Terascon primitive work, Tepan, Toltec and Aztec, each in its turn, had reached an interesting state of development in Old Mexico; for these people had learned to handle metals, precious and semi-precious stones, rocks, burnt and dried earths, lumber, etc., and constructed from them objects of unique beauty.

3

Within recent years, while excavating at Azcapotzalco the writer came upon many curious little statuettes, so droll in their conception that it is impossible not to believe that the old Mexicans, also, must have had a well developed sense of humor which helped to carry them over hard places.

The Spaniards destroyed all they came across with ruthless

TOLTEC SPECIMENS EXCAVATED AT AZCAPOTZALCO
THE FREEDOM THAT INSPIRED THE MAKERS OF THESE FIGURINES SEEMS ALSO TO
HAVE INSPIRED THE SPANIARDS LATER

hands, but they could not remain unaffected by the existing work they found, and the influence of the early Mexican art is easily seen in the Spaniards' first efforts in construction on a new soil.

Due to the climate and the limited amount of skilled labor, and the materials available, it was natural that structures should have plain surfaces full of irregularities due to having been built by hand. But it was characteristic of the Spaniard that he embellished profusely with both carving and color whenever an excuse offered.

AN ARCHITECTURAL PILGRIMAGE

In spite of the destruction that Mexico has experienced during the last century, there still exists every few miles a church or historic building frequently surrounded with nothing but a few Indian huts.

MISSION OF SAN JOSE DE AGUAYO, SAN ANTONIO, TEXAS

ARCHES HERE WERE USED IN PLACE OF BEAMS AND FORMED A PERMANENT AND RELIABLE BACKGROUND FOR ALL FORMS OF EMBELLISHMENT

Here we find the main building composed of intensely interesting hand moulded surfaces, often with the richest of windows or doors, cornices, and quoins, towers or parapets, and it is not uncommon to find these latter constructed of an entirely different material from the remainder of the building. In outlying districts, and even in big cities, adobe blocks covered with stucco form the main structure. The ornamental portions were made of a soft stone called

Tepetate, a porous stone that hardens with the atmosphere and be-comes almost a solid piece, and which was set slightly in advance of the general wall surface.

Colonnettes, capitals, mouldings, and domes in most unusual color effects abound everywhere, and the result was obtained partly by pigments and partly by tiles, as bizarre and unexpected as any-thing that has come out of Russia, Austria, or France. With the re-sult that such richness of effect exists nowhere else on the North American Continent and age has only added to its charm.

The outstanding features of this fascinating period of architecture evolved by these ancient Spaniards are the open arcades (porches we call them) and the large unbroken surfaces which form the mass of the wall between the elaborate and often most artistic surrounds to the doors and windows. No matter how unusual or elaborate this enrichment might become, however, it always had a foil in the unbroken wall surfaces which provided the essential contrast.

Panelled doors of unique character (the latter without finish as we understand varnish or paint), delicate metal balconies, iron and wooden grilles, helped to make up a style of architecture so free, so largely suited to our temperament and needs, that it would seem as if the "American point of view" had found its expression in archi-tecture on this continent centuries ago, in this group of educated Spaniards who desired to design in beauty and construct in truth.

The reason that the buildings below the Rio Grande, though built by one of the Latin races centuries ago, seem so aptly to fit our American needs is not hard to understand.

The climate of the higher portions of Mexico is very similar to that of the United States, sunlight and fresh air are in abundance and large windows, open porches and wide-spreading rooms are essential. In turn these express the temperament of the American people with its heartiness and warmth, freedom and, one might add, sense of humor and unconventionality, better than any cold, dignified classical building ever could.

The American country home, perhaps the most thoroughly appointed of any in the world, has been largely adopted from styles of architecture primarily unsuited to this climate, and to the mode of living of its occupants. The ideal house should be a portrait of the life lived within its four walls. Colonial houses, charming to a degree, invariably possess a satisfying regularity, but this sometimes leads to an austerity of feeling and difficulties in the internal arrangements. Windows often do not fit into the most desirable places in the rooms. The ceilings frequently are low, making the rooms far warmer than it is desirable to have them, and though such difficulties may be largely overcome when handled by a trained designer, the style does present limitations.

Our ancestors in England with their exquisite Tudor houses had no need for a practical porch or a big window that allowed the free circulation of air so vitally important on an August day. Their need was to overcome the difficulties of a damp climate—and the exclusion of the rain and the weather was far more important than to provide access for the breezes and the sunlight.

Speaking architecturally Italian regularity and French whimsicality are both ideal in their particular sphere, but when adapted to the American home they can be deficient in many respects, due to having been the outgrowth of entirely different controlling conditions.

But the buildings in Mexico, with the slightest adaptation to fit them for twentieth century requirements, do comply with American needs in a manner rarely equalled by any other style of architecture.

Freedom is apparent in their construction. Rules with the old

Spaniard were made only for the use of those who could not dare for themselves without exterior guidance, so they paid little heed to them but bent their knowledge of these to their own advantage. If the spacing between the columns on the arcade or the precise regularity of the windows upon the façade did not produce a desirable treatment on the interior arrangement of the building, the columns or windows were frankly moved, usually by a master hand, and the result was an interesting composition. Hard regularity was supplanted by charming irregularity in most instances.

Again, should the main entrance not logically develop in the center of the building, it wasn't put there. The interior of the structure was seldom arbitrarily distorted to enable some theoretical architectural principle to be maintained.

The great American hotel with its multitudes of windows, its airy foyers and ball-rooms, pent-houses, towers and roof-gardens, seems instinctively to demand the use of a type of architecture as elastic in treatment as that found in Mexico. The towering office building with its dominating vertical lines, and nothing to relieve its great surfaces, except the piercing of innumerable holes to form windows, can be designed after Mexican ideas with a success not easily obtained in forms that must maintain fixed characteristics with a rigid regularity. This would apply especially in the adaptions necessary to buildings constructed under new zoning laws, which regulate the projection of cornices, height, water tables, size of dormers, etc.

American architecture undoubtedly will take its place in the world upon its commercial buildings, and the design of these is rapidly taking the path that the materials composing them require. Forms defined by the use of steel or concrete faced with some readily handled materials, which can be tied on to this frame, such as thin slabs of stone, brick, stucco, or terra cotta, are creating the dominant features of skyscraper architecture.

The introduction of color by the use of burnt clays, terra cotta or faiences, all of which are capable of reproduction at comparatively small cost, is fast forming an ornamental feature of the greatest buildings of the country, and it was in instinct the same theory that controlled the work in Mexico years ago.

America is a commercial nation with very strong artistic tendencies, but commercial buildings have to be commercial; competition has made them so. A building is a financial undertaking, and beauty, though essential, is subservient within reason to the production of revenue in money or happiness.

An investor will not put additional capital into a structure merely for the sake of maintaining some architectural lines, unless he really sees a definite return from so doing. A building must be constructed of the best possible material to withstand wear and tear, but it must also be designed in a manner that will bring in a revenue commensurate with the amount of investment, and this is obtained not only through the artistic merit of the building, but also through its desirability and the facilities it offers.

We are in an age of change and the possibilities of altering or adding to the existing building should be considered, primarily, in almost any design today. Few buildings laid out on the purest classical lines will allow such additions without having the appearance of the proverbial sore thumb.

Mexican architectural irregularities add a charm, and the style actually provides most readily the vehicle for possible alterations.

If the relations between the governments had not been estranged the buildings of that land of architectural charm in the south would already have been the prototype of a most popular style of architecture here. Southern California has already taken hold of it and within the next few years, as the intercourse between the two countries increases, the abounding advantages of Mexican work to fill American requirements will unquestionably compel its consideration more and more in almost every type of building.

EL OBISPADO, MONTERREY, MEXICO

PLATES

Plate II

CHURCH OF EL SALTO DEL AGUA, MEXICO CITY

THE UNEXPECTED ORNAMENT WHILE OFTEN NOT BEAUTIFUL IS ALWAYS
INTERESTING AND QUITE FREQUENTLY REFRESHING

Plate III

SCHOOL BUILT FOR THE ORPHANS OF IMPOVERISHED NOBLE FAMILIES

ARCHITECTURAL ADVANTAGE CAN BE TAKEN OF THE SURROUND TO
AN OPENING TO GIVE STRENGTH TO AN ENTIRE GROUPING

Plate IV

AN INTERESTING NOTE AGAINST THE SKYLINE—A SCALLOPED PARAPET

Plate V

CALLE ESCALERILLAS

SHOWING A VARIED TREATMENT OF FAÇADES AND WALLS. THE CORNICE
ELIMINATED AND STRING COURSE ONLY USED

Plate VI

THE WALL TREATMENT HERE MAKES A CORNICE UNNECESSARY

Plate VII

DELICATE BALCONIES AND GRACEFUL WATERSPOUTS ARE AN EASY METHOD OF
ADDING CHARM TO THE PLAINEST BUILDINGS

Plate VIII

A HOUSE IN THE CITY OF MEXICO

PANELLING IN STUCCO IS NOT UNKNOWN TO THE MEXICANS

Plate IX

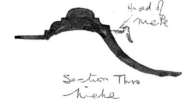

THE RELIEF OF PLAIN WALL SURFACES IS
DELIGHTFULLY ACHIEVED BY THE USE
OF NICHES OR WALL PANELS

SOFT WHITE STONE FORMS THE NICHE
IT IS SET IN THE RED BURNT CLAY THAT
FORMS THE GENERAL WALL SURFACE

Plate X

A HOUSE IN MEXICO CITY

A CRESTING TREATMENT THAT COULD EASILY BE DEVELOPED
IN TERRA COTTA

STUCCO SURFACE AND MODELLING PROVIDES CHARM FOR THE
SIMPLEST COMPOSITION

Plate XI

CALLE REGINA, MEXICO CITY

THE WALLS AND DETAILS OF THIS TENEMENT ARE FULL OF QUAINT CHARM

Plate XII

DIGNITY ACHIEVED WITH LITTLE HEIGHT

LAS VIZCAINAS

HERE TWO COLORED MATERIALS EMPHASIZE THE LINES OF THE COMPOSITION

Plate XIII

OUR STREET CORNERS COULD BE IMPROVED BY GREATER INTEREST IN THE ANGLES OF OUR BUILDINGS

Plate XIV

A STUCCO FACADE IN LOW RELIEF, MEXICO CITY

A DELIGHTFUL CORNICE ON A HOUSE ON THE AVENIDA BOLÍVAR, MEXICO CITY

Plate XV

THE CORNER OF A BUILDING, MEXICO CITY, NOW USED FOR A STORE
IT IS IN TWO-COLORED STONE WORK

Plate XVI

JOCKEY CLUB, MEXICO CITY

HERE COLORED TILE AND CARVING BLEND TO PRODUCE
THE MAXIMUM OF RICHNESS

Plate XVII

NATIONAL LIBRARY, MEXICO CITY

THE MEXICANS DID NOT ALWAYS USE AN UNLIMITED AMOUNT OF DETAIL

Plate XVIII

HOTEL ITURBIDE, CITY OF MEXICO

THE CHANGING OF FENESTRATION AT DIFFERENT FLOOR LEVELS HELD
NO DIFFICULTY FOR THE MEXICAN

Plate XIX

FEDERAL PALACE, AGUAS CALIENTES, MEXICO

SURFACE MODELLING HAS BEEN CARRIED TO AN EXTREME

Plate XX

WHERE PORTALES FACE THE ALAMEDA

Plate XXI

A TWO-STORIED DOORWAY WILL FREQUENTLY
GIVE DIGNITY TO THE SIMPLEST FAÇADE

STORES UNDER AN ARCADE, MEXICO CITY

NOTICE THE INTERESTING CAPITALS

Plate XXII

CHURCH AT GUANAJUATO, MEXICO

Plate XXIII

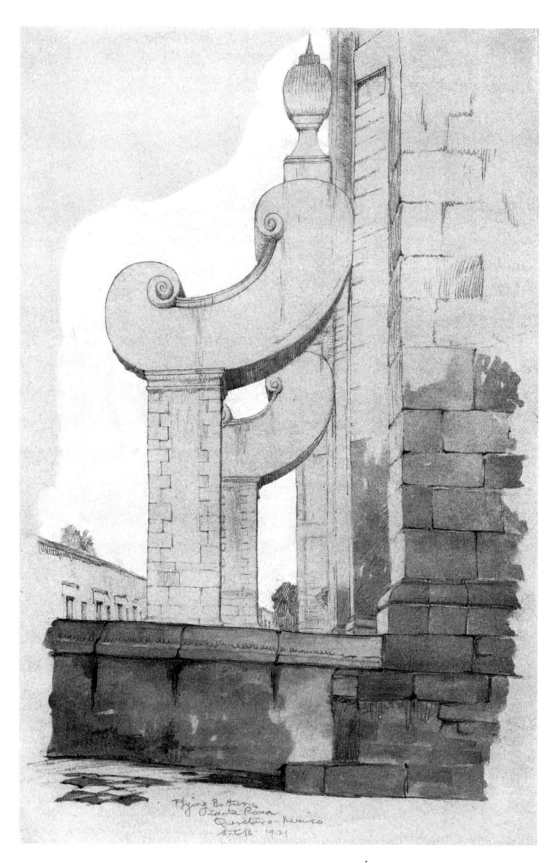

FLYING BUTTRESS—SANTA ROSA, QUERÉTARO, MEXICO

Plate XXIV

BUILDING IN TEPOZOTLÁN

IT WOULD MAKE AN EFFECTIVE DESIGN FOR A GARAGE

STAIRWAY UP THE HILL IN GUADALUPE

Plate XXV

A CHURCH WALL SHRINE, CHURUBUSCO

A RICH SPOT IN THE MIDST OF CRUDE SURROUNDINGS

A WALL TABLET, MEXICO CITY

A SHORT HISTORICAL NOTE RELIEVES
THE SEVERITY OF THIS WALL

ON THE ROAD TO SAN JUAN

TEOTIHUACAN—GARDEN

WALL WITH POSTS

Plate XXVI

AN ELABORATELY CARVED AQUEDUCT FOUNTAIN NEAR CHAPULTEPEC

Plate XXVII

THERE IS A SUGGESTION FOR A GARDEN WALL IN THIS CURIOUSLY
BUILT OLD WALL AROUND THE CHURCH OF TACUBA

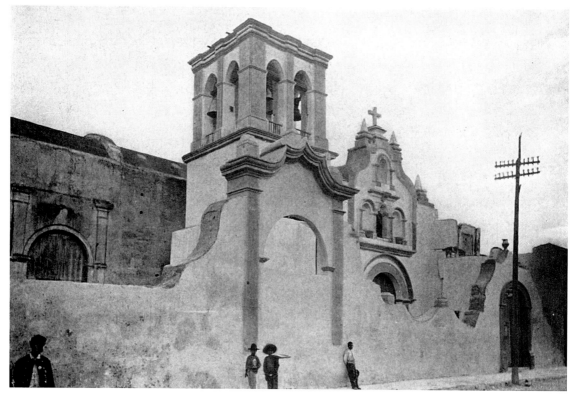

WALL OF THE CHURCH OF SAN FRANCISCO, MONTERREY

Plate XXVIII

EL CHORRO, SAN MIGUEL DE ALLENDE, MEXICO—GARDEN WALLS WITH LEDGES FOR GROWING PLANTS

Plate XXIX

THE CAMPANILE OF SAN GABRIEL MISSION, LOS ANGELES, CALIFORNIA.
WINDOWS IN THE PLACE OF BELLS AND HARMONY WOULD STILL EXIST

Plate XXX

COURTYARD OF THE CONVENT AT CHURUBUSCO

Plate XXXI

WELL IN THE COURT OF AN ANCIENT CONVENT IN MEXICO

Plate XXXII

PATIO GARDEN, SANTA BARBARA MISSION, CALIFORNIA

PATIO DEL CONVENTO

HOW A FOUNTAIN CAN HELP A SMALL GARDEN

Plate XXXIII

OLD BISHOP'S PALACE, MONTERREY

A FARM PATIO, A FARM-YARD WITH REAL INDIVIDUALITY

Plate XXXIV

PATIO, COLEGIO DE LAS VIZCAINAS

COURTYARD OF THE HOTEL ITURBIDE

SUMMER HOTELS MIGHT WELL FOLLOW THESE EXAMPLES OF
OUR MEXICAN COUSINS

Plate XXXV

SANTA BARBARA MISSION, CALIFORNIA

Plate XXXVI

AN ARCHED STREET IN AMECAMECA

ENTRANCE TO THE SEPULCRO, SACRO MONTE, AMECAMECA

Plate XXXVII

OLD GATEWAY, ORIZABA, MEXICO

A LAND DEVELOPMENT WITH THIS AS AN ENTRANCE WOULD AT
ONCE ACQUIRE DISTINCTION

PICTURESQUE LODGINGS FOR MAN AND BEAST, MEXICO CITY

Plate XXXVIII

IXTLACIHUATL FROM PLAZA, AMECAMECA

GATEWAY WITH A DOUBLE ARCH, COYOACÁN

Plate XXXIX

ENTRANCE TO THE GROUNDS OF SAN LUIS REY DE FRANCIA,
SAN DIEGO, CALIFORNIA

A STUCCO GARDEN WALL MAY EASILY ADD DELIGHT TO A BARREN SPOT

Plate XL

DETAIL
OF
PIERCED
BALUSTRADE

SECTION
THRU
BALUSTRADE
&
CORNICE

DETAIL OF
BRONZE
ORNAMENT
ON SPOUT
OF GARGOYLE

STUCCO

SOFT
STONE

SKETCHED ELEVATION
OF CORNER OF
BUILDING.
MEXICO CITY
1921

ENRICH THE ANGLES AND THE WALLS WILL TAKE CARE OF THEMSELVES

Plate XLI

A RICH CORNER, MEXICO CITY

EL PARQUE DEL CONDE, MEXICO CITY

ONE SUCH SPOT CAN MAKE AN ENTIRE FAÇADE

Plate XLII

A GARGOYLE DEFTLY EMPLOYED WILL GIVE RELIEF TO THE FLATTEST FAÇADE

A PARAPET WITH A GARGOYLE MAKES THE CONVENTIONAL CORNICE UNNECESSARY

Plate XLIII

OLD MEXICO DID NOT USE TERRA COTTA BUT IF IT HAD THE FACTORIES
WOULD CERTAINLY HAVE WORKED OVERTIME

Plate XLIV

INDIVIDUALITY MAY BE DEVELOPED IN ANY BUILDING IF ALL
ITS ENRICHMENT HAS SOME DEFINITE MEANING

Plate XLV

FLYING SAILS, GUADALUPE

A TOWER THOUGH ALWAYS IN SIGHT DOES
NOT HAVE TO BE CONVENTIONAL

Plate XLVI

CHURCHYARD, TZINTZUNTZÁN, MEXICO

WHEN A TOWER STANDS UP TO THE SKY GIVE IT SUPPORT

Plate XLVII

THE PALACIO FEDERAL, QUERÉTARO, MEXICO

THE TOWER AND BALCONY ABOVE THE PATIO CARRY
RICHNESS TO THE Nth POWER

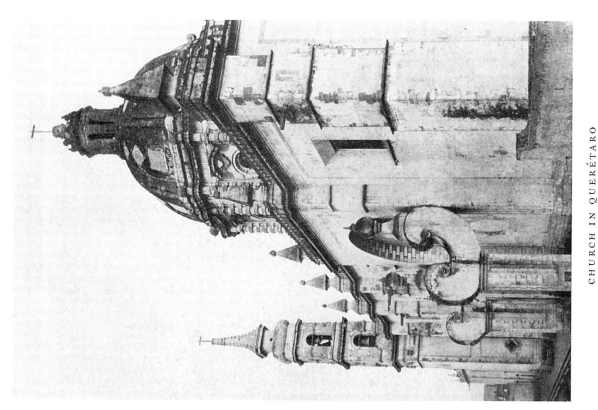

CHURCH IN QUERÉTARO

A STALWART BUTTRESS GIVES THE SENSE
OF STRENGTH TO A STRUCTURE

Plate XLVIII

SAN JOSÉ, SAN ANTONIO, TEXAS

BUILT TO CARRY DOWN THROUGH THE AGES

Plate XLIX

SANTO DOMINGO CHURCH, CITY OF MEXICO

Plate L

BELFRY AND CLOCK TOWERS OF THE CATHEDRAL
OF MORELIA, MEXICO

TWIN SENTINELS OF GRACE

BELFRY OF THE CHURCH OF SAN FELIPE,
GUADALAJARA

THE TOWER STANDS EVER ON GUARD

Plate LI

SANTO DOMINGO, PORTAL AND CHURCH, MEXICO

A FITTING CONTRAST AT THE END OF SUCH A COLONNADE

Plate LII

PORCH AND FOUNTAIN OF SACRO MONTE, AMECAMECA

VIEW IN JALAPA, VERA CRUZ

AN EXTERIOR ENTRANCE TO AN UPPER STORY CAN BE
MADE A SOURCE OF ADDED CHARM

Plate LIII

CORRIDORS OF SAN JUAN BAUTISTA MISSION, CALIFORNIA

CORRIDORS OF MEXICALCINGO, MEXICO CITY

Plate LIV

SAN FERNANDO MISSION

HOW COOL FOR A PORCH, PUBLIC OR PRIVATE

STREET IN AGUAS CALIENTES, MEXICO

THERE ARE MANY GARDENS AND COUNTRY HOUSES THAT WOULD BE
GREATLY IMPROVED BY SUCH AN ADDITION

Plate LV

A STREET IN EL ORO, MEXICO

THE HOUSE ON THE HILL CAN CARRY ITS PORCHES WITH IT

Plate LVI

CORRIDOR AT SAN JUAN CAPISTRANO MISSION, CALIFORNIA, WITH
ARCHED COLUMNS AND HEAVILY BEAMED CEILING

A MEXICAN HACIENDA CORRIDOR

THE TRUE THRESHOLD OF THE GARDEN

Plate LVII

CORRIDOR IN THE FRANCISCAN MONASTERY, TEPOZOTLÁN

CONVENTO DEL CARMEN, COYOACÁN

A TREATMENT SUITABLE FOR SLEEPING PORCHES

Plate LVIII

STREET MARKET IN PUEBLA, MEXICO

PORCHES ARE NOT LIMITED TO FLAT CEILINGS

RARE ARCHITECTURE IN PUEBLA, MEXICO

A WEDDING CAKE NO LESS!

Plate LIX

CORRIDOR OF A HOUSE AT MITLA

THE COUNTRY HOUSE PORCH, THE LINK BETWEEN THE HOUSE AND THE GARDEN

Plate LX

CORTEZ HOUSE, COYOACÁN, MEXICO—A PORCH TO BE SUCCESSFUL MUST BE OPEN AND AIRY

Plate LXI

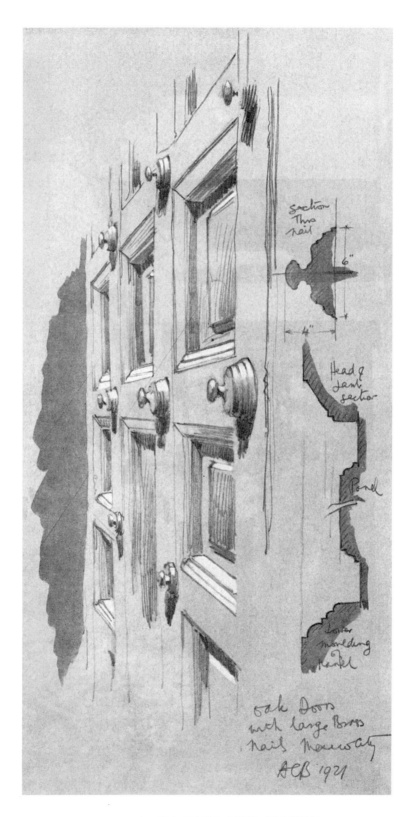

HOW A FEW BIG NAILS LEND DIGNITY
TO A DOOR OPENING

Plate LXII

DOOR OF THE CHURCH OF SAN FRANCISCO,
SAN ANTONIO

GARDEN DOORWAY OF THE MISSION OF
SAN BUENAVENTURA

Plate LXIII

A STUDY IN CONTRASTS

CHURCH BUILT BY A SUCCESSFUL SILVER MINER IN 1757 AND DEDICATED
TO SAN SEBASTIAN—Y—SANTA PRISCA, TAXCO

Plate LXIV

SAN JOSÉ, SAN ANTONIO, TEXAS

OBVIOUSLY THERE IS NO RESTRAINT TO THE FANCY HERE

Plate LXV

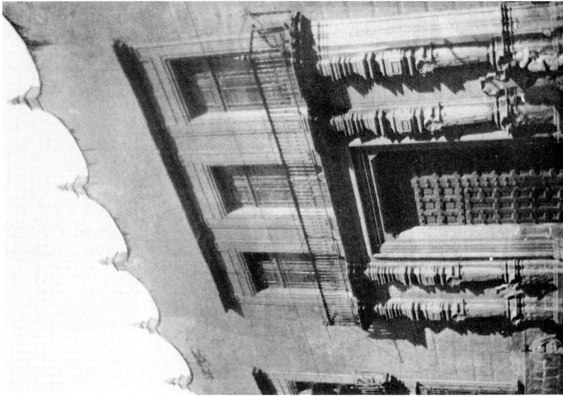

IF THE DOOR IS NOT LARGE ENOUGH FOR THE
COMPOSITION ADD MORE SURROUNDING FEATURES

THE SETTLEMENT OF THE BUILDING HAS HIDDEN THE
BOTTOM OF THE DOOR BELOW THE GRADE

Plate LXVI

DOOR OF SAN JOSÉ, SAN ANTONIO, TEXAS

THE APPROACH TO THE DOORWAY MAY ADD LARGELY TO ITS IMPORTANCE

Plate LXVII

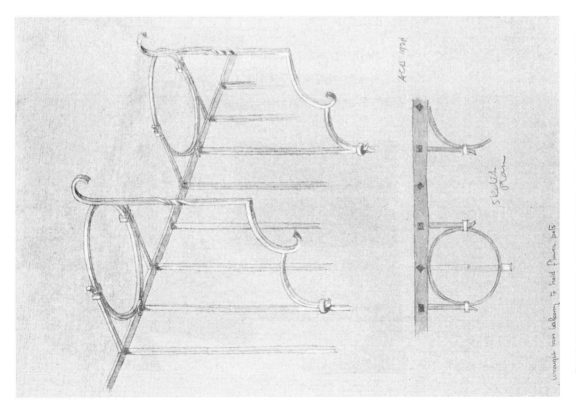

BRONZE WHEEL GUARD, MEXICO CITY

THE MEXICANS USED METAL LAVISHLY

WROUGHT IRON BALCONIES TO HOLD FLOWER POTS

THEY ADD TO THE PICTURESQUENESS

OF THE FAÇADE

Plate LXVIII

DOORWAY AND BALCONY WITH
INTRICATE CARVINGS

ENTRANCE TO THE HOTEL ITURBIDE, MEXICO CITY

THE DOORWAY IS THE MOST IMPORTANT FEATURE OF A STRUCTURE AND
ITS FLANKING MEMBERS CAN EITHER MAKE OR MAR IT

Plate LXIX

DIFFERENT TYPES OF NAILS CHANGE THE CHARACTER
OF A DOOR AS MUCH AS DIFFERENT TYPES OF
MOLDINGS CAN CHANGE A CORNICE

Plate LXX

STUCCO DOORWAY AND NICHE AT SAN GABRIEL
MISSION, CALIFORNIA

Plate LXXI

THE CEMETERY DOOR, SANTA BÁRBARA

A SIMPLE DOORWAY, MEXICO CITY

Plate LXXII

ENTRANCE TO THE MISSION, SAN ANTONIO, TEXAS

Plate LXXIII

EL CARMEN, SAN LUIS POTOSÍ, MEXICO CITY

AN EXAMPLE OF A SENSE OF SCALE AND STRENGTH GAINED BY CONTRASTING
APPLIED ORNAMENT UPON SOLIDITY

FIRST SHRINE, MEXICO CITY

ONE SPOT OF DETAIL MAKES THE WHOLE COMPOSITION

Plate LXXIV

IRON WORK IMITATED IN STONE HAS AN
UNNATURAL CHARACTER

SIMPLE FORMS DISPOSED WITH CARE MAKE THIS
BLIND GABLE LIVE WITH INTEREST

Plate LXXV

DOORWAY OF THE FORMER BISHOP'S PALACE

I USED TO GO IN HERE TO GET

MY SHOES SHINED

OLD DOORWAY OF SAN LUIS REY MISSION, CALIFORNIA

A DOORWAY WITHIN A DOORWAY MAKES THE

COMPOSITION FIT ITS SPACE

Plate LXXVI

FRONT OF THE CATHEDRAL, MEXICO CITY

HERE STRENGTH AND DELICACY STAND SIDE BY SIDE IN PERFECT HARMONY

Plate LXXVII

THE ALAMO WAS IMMORTALIZED BY THE MEN WHO FOUGHT ON THE HALLOWED GROUNDS

Plate LXXVIII

SUCCESSFUL COMPOSITIONS CAN BE MADE BY CONTRASTING LINES OR CONTRASTING
TREATMENTS OF SURFACES WITH EQUAL SUCCESS

Plate LXXIX

CHURCH OF THE BLACK CHRIST, VERA CRUZ

CARVING IS NOT ESSENTIAL TO A SUCCESSFUL DESIGN

OLDEST CHURCH IN MEXICO (TLAXCALA)

BY USING A SUITABLE DARK MATERIAL FOR THE DOORS THE OUT-
LINE OF THE GREATER OPENING IS UNAFFECTED AND YET
ONLY THE SMALL DOORS BELOW ARE USED

Plate LXXX

SANTA MÓNICA, GUADALAJARA

WHEN CONTRASTS SATISFY THEY ARE THEIR

OWN JUSTIFICATION

IGLESIA DEL CARMEN, SAN LUIS POTOSÍ

THE RESTLESSNESS OF THE OVER BROKEN LINE

IS DISTINCTLY EVIDENT HERE

Plate LXXXI

COLEGIO DE LAS VIZCAYNAS, MEXICO CITY—A PLAYFUL RESTRAINT ADDS MUCH CHARM

Plate LXXXII

THE SHAPES ARCHITECTURAL FORMS MAY TAKE ARE WITHOUT NUMBER

Plate LXXXIII

THE SPANIARDS COULD MIX MANY MATERIALS
WITH FREEDOM AND HARMONY

Plate LXXXIV

THE FREEST CARVING IF DOMINATED BY A DEFINITE STRUCTURAL
FORM AUTOMATICALLY FALLS BACK INTO ITS PROPER PLACE

Plate LXXXV

IF THE JOINTS OF THE STONE WORK DID NOT SUIT,
NEW LINES WERE CUT TO OBTAIN THE
DESIRED SENSE OF SCALE

SHOULD THE INTERIOR MAKE IT DESIRABLE TO HAVE
WINDOWS OF DIFFERENT HEIGHTS SIDE BY SIDE,
THE MEXICAN FRANKLY ARRANGED IT SO

Plate LXXXVI

THE MEXICAN WAS NO MORE BOUND TO TRADITION THAN THE AMERICAN IS TODAY

Plate LXXXVII

MAIN ENTRANCE AND INDEPENDENCE BELL,
NATIONAL PALACE, MEXICO CITY

THERE IS NO LIMIT TO THE SPREAD OF A
DOORWAY SURROUND

WHEN THE MEXICAN DECIDED THAT HE WISHED A
CERTAIN FORM OF ORNAMENT IN A CERTAIN
PLACE, HE BENT HIS ARCHITECTURAL
LINES TO ACCOMMODATE IT

Plate LXXXVIII

JUST A PLAIN DOORWAY, BALCONY, AND WINDOW—THE
SHADOWS DO THE REST

Plate LXXXIX

THE MEXICAN GAVE HIS WINDOWS ARCHITRAVES OR OMITTED THEM ACCORDING TO HIS DESIRE

Plate XC

IF YOU ORNAMENT ONE MAIN FEATURE SUFFICIENTLY
YOU NEED NOT ORNAMENT ELSEWHERE

Plate XCI

SUN DIAL AND PARAPET SHOWING A TREATMENT COMPOSED OF CURVED
ADOBE BLOCKS—COULD BE BUILT OF CLAY ANYWHERE

Plate XCII

IRREGULARITY BEGETS INTEREST

NARROW STREETS, GUANAJUATO

Plate XCIII

CASA DE ALVARADO, COYOACÁN, WITH POINTED BALCONY RAILINGS
AND DECORATIONS IN LOW RELIEF, A PLEASING SIMILARITY

Plate XCIV

A SECOND STORY IRON BALCONY CAN
HAVE ITS FLOWERS AND YET
NOT DETRACT FROM THE
AVAILABLE SPACE

BALCONY ON THE ROOF OF THE JOCKEY CLUB, MEXICO CITY

THIS LIGHT IRON RAILING IN NO WAY DETRACTS FROM
THE IMPORTANCE OF THE STONE FINISH

Plate XCV

STREET CORNER, CUERNAVACA

AN OPEN ANGLE TREATMENT BUT STILL MAINTAINING THE REQUIRED DEGREE OF SOLIDITY

Plate XCVI

BALCONIES HERE SUPPLY PROTECTION BUT DO NOT INTRUDE
UPON THE ARCHITECTURAL LINE

Plate XCVII

CURIOUS CARVINGS ON THE PALACIO FEDERAL, QUERÉTARO, MEXICO

Plate XCVIII

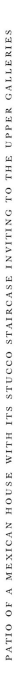

PATIO OF A MEXICAN HOUSE WITH ITS STUCCO STAIRCASE INVITING TO THE UPPER GALLERIES

Plate XCIX

EL CALVARIO, TEHUACÁN, PUEBLA, MEXICO, WITH ITS WIDE LOW STAIRWAY

WHAT A DELIGHTFUL ENTRANCE TO A FORMAL GARDEN

Plate C

SUBIDA AL SANTUARIO, VILLA DE GUADALUPE

WHO COULD RESIST THE TEMPTATION TO CLIMB UP?

STAIRWAY IN A STREET IN GUANAJUATO, MEXICO

NOT PRACTICAL BUT VERY PICTURESQUE

Plate CI

SAN GABRIEL MISSION, PASADENA, CALIFORNIA

THE GENUINE SPIRIT OF THE OLD WORLD IS AT OUR VERY DOORSTEP

Plate CII

WITH THE GREAT IMPORTANCE OF STORES ON THE STREET LEVEL OF
HOTELS AND BANK BUILDINGS, SUCH AN ENTRANCE
HAS A PECULIAR INTEREST

Plate CIII

A VERY UNUSUAL FORM OF ORNAMENT

WOODEN PANEL CARVED IN LOW RE-
LIEF, DOOR OF THE CONVENT OF
CUAUHTITLÁN, A. D. 1538

LARGE DOORS, MEXICO CITY

MANY SMALL PANELS REMOVE THE
AUSTERITY OF THE LARGEST DOORS

Plate CIV

RUINS OF THE CONVENT OF SAN FRANCISCO, ZACATECAS

Plate CV

THE MOTIF IS HERE OF MANY THINGS THAT COULD BE MADE USE OF IN A HOTEL BALL-ROOM

Plate CVI

TILED WAINSCOTING

TILES CAN BRING COLOR TO AN OTHERWISE DREARY SPOT

Plate CVII

JOCKEY CLUB, MEXICO CITY

FOUNTAIN AND BALCONIES OF AN INTERIOR COURTYARD

Plate CVIII

HOTEL DILIGENCIAS, PUEBLA (LA COCINA — THE KITCHEN)

SUCH A BRACKETED WALL TREATMENT HOLDS OUT MANY POSSIBILITIES

INTERIOR OF LIVING ROOM, ESTUDILLO HOUSE

KITCHEN OF ESTUDILLO HOUSE, SAN DIEGO

Plate CIX

THE COLORED CEILING AGAINST THE PLAIN WALL IS A MOST
SUCCESSFUL DEPARTURE FROM THE OLD COLORED
WALLS WITH WHITE CEILINGS

Plate CX

INTERIORS OF OLD MISSIONS, CALIFORNIA